C000096301

PBR

A Pillar Box Red Publication

in association with

MATCH! & WorldSoccer

ISBN: 978-1-912456-78-9

Photographs: © Getty Images.

RANGERS 2021

Written by
Ben Wier

Edited by
Sam Straw

Designed by
Darryl Tooth

AN INDEPENDENT PRODUCTION

CONTENTS

CLUB HISTORY

RANGERS THROUGH THE YEARS!

GLASGOW FA!

Founded in 1883, the Glasgow Football Association is one of the oldest footy bodies ever! Rangers, Queen's Park, Third Lanark, Northern, Partick, Clyde, and Pollokshields Athletic all attended its first committee meeting!

1883

FIRST OLD FIRM FIXTURE!

In 1887, arch-rivals Celtic were founded, with the first fixture between the two Glasgow sides taking place in 1888! The match was only a friendly, with a Celtic side mainly made up of guest players from Hibernian winning 5-2!

1888

RANGERS' BIRTH!

Four men formed Rangers way back in March 1872 – Peter Campbell, William McBeath and brothers Moses and Peter McNeil. The quartet were keen rowers, but decided to create a footy team after seeing a group of men playing football on Glasgow Green's Flesher's Haugh!

1881

1872

1890

From the beginning, The Gers' shirts have been all blue, with white shorts too! The name Rangers is believed to have come from an English rugby team called Swindon Rangers!

CLUB CREST!

Footy historians reckon the current Rangers badge seen on the 2020-21 shirts was created when the club was formed back in 1872! The oldest remaining piece of club memorabilia with the crest on it is from the 1881-82 season, though!

SCOTLAND'S FIRST LEAGUE CHAMPS!

1890 was a big year for Rangers – by this point, they were playing in the Ibrox area of Glasgow and then became one of the ten teams taking part in the first-ever Scottish Football League season! Of course, The Gers bagged the title – sharing the honours with Dumbarton after an end-of-season play-off ended 2-2!

SCOTTISH CUP WINNERS!

Three years after becoming league champions, Rangers bagged their first-ever Scottish Cup! In the 1894 final, The Gers beat Celtic 3-1!

IBROX DISASTER

In January 1971, 66 football fans sadly lost their lives at the end of a Rangers game against Celtic, when barriers collapsed. Scottish football clubs regularly mark the anniversary of the disaster by holding minute silences before fixtures in January.

1971

YEARS OF DOMINANCE!

By the time the 1930s came around, Rangers were one of the dominant forces in Scottish football! The Gers had bagged 17 league titles, and won the Scottish Cup five times. Bonkers!

1949

1972

1930

1894

EUROPEAN CUP WINNERS' CUP TRIUMPH!

Rangers first competed in European football back in 1956, but they had to wait until 1972 to taste success! In 1961, they lost to Fiorentina in the European Cup Winners' Cup final, then lost the 1967 final to Bayern Munich! They finally bagged the trophy in 1972, though - beating Dynamo Moscow at the Nou Camp!

1899

IBROX OPENS!

Rangers originally played at a ground to the east of the current stadium, and it wasn't until 1899 when Ibrox Stadium actually opened. Then called Ibrox Park, it had an initial capacity of 40,000 spectators!

THE TREBLE!

Over 75 years after they were formed, Rangers became the first team in Scottish football to bag a domestic treble! The Ibrox giants pipped Dundee to the title by a point, and got their hands on both the Scottish Cup and League Cup!

SCOTLAND'S FIRST MILLION-POUND PLAYER!

After bagging the 1986-87 league title, the Glasgow giants splashed out £1.5 million on Tottenham defender Richard Gough! This was a big deal in 1987, as no Scottish club had ever spent that much on a player before!

NINE IN A ROW!

Between 1988 and 1997, Rangers won the league title nine times in a row! In doing so, they equalled the same record set by Celtic back in the 1970s! Souness left just before winning the third title, with legendary gaffer Walter Smith replacing him and bagging the rest!

1997

McCOIST SIGNS!

In 1983, Rangers signed Ally McCoist from Sunderland for a bargain £185,000! In his first 10 seasons, the lethal finisher was the club's top goalscorer eight times, including one campaign where he hit 49 goals in all comps! Ally left the club in 1998 as The Gers' record goalscorer, bagging 355 goals in total! He won 20 trophies as a player at Ibrox, too!

1992

1994

1987

1986

1983

BEST OF BRITISH!

In 1992, the European Cup was revamped as the Champions League, and Rangers were the first British team to play a match in the new competition! The Gers had an epic run in Europe that season, beating Leeds in the Second Round! They were one win from the final too, but failed to beat CSKA Moscow!

SOUNESS ARRIVES!

In 1985-86, Rangers had four different managers and finished 5th in the league, 15 points behind Celtic! The fourth different gaffer was Graeme Souness, who joined the club as player-manager. The following season, the Scotland legend guided Rangers to the league title and the Scottish League Cup. What an impact!

SUPERSTAR SIGNINGS!

The Glasgow giants were big players in the 90s transfer market! Euro 92 winner Brian Laudrup joined from Fiorentina in 1994 for £2.3 million, then a year later England hero Paul Gascoigne signed for £4.3 million from Lazio! The world's best players wanted to play at Ibrox!

2003 saw Rangers pip Celtic to the title on goal difference, beat them in the Scottish League Cup final, and claim a seventh domestic treble – a record The Hoops still haven't beaten today!

OFF-PITCH PAIN!

On February 14, 2012, Rangers were placed into administration after hitting financial trouble. The club was instantly docked 10 points, but worse was to come. By the end of the season, Rangers had gone bust and were relegated to the fourth tier of Scottish football.

2012

TOP-FLIGHT RETURN!

Four years later, and Rangers were back in the big time! Club legend Ally McCoist was in charge as the club won promotion two seasons in a row between 2012 and 2014, then Mark Warburton finished the job after winning the 2016 Scottish Championship title!

2003

2008

2016

EUROPA LEAGUE RUN!

Panathinaikos, Werder Bremen, Sporting Lisbon and Fiorentina were all brushed aside, as Rangers marched all the way to the 2008 Europa League Final! Zenit beat them to the trophy in Manchester though, with former manager Dick Advocaat in charge of the Russian giants!

CLASSIC
RANGERS
MOMENTS
NO. 1

THE GAZZA GAME!

RANGERS — 3
Gascoigne 21, 80, 86 (pen)

ABERDEEN — 1
Irvine 19

Date: April 28, 1996

Stadium: Ibrox Stadium, Glasgow

Competition: Scottish Premiership

What happened? This game is remembered for one thing – Paul Gascoigne's magical treble that bagged Rangers the Scottish Prem for the eighth season in a row! After exchanging goals early on through Brian Irvine and Gazza, the England legend hit the decisive strike 10 minutes from time when he dribbled from his own half all the way to The Dons' penalty box to fire home! It was a sick solo strike, with Gazza scoring a penalty six minutes later to secure the match, his hat-trick and the league title!

FOLLOW MATCH!

FOR ALL THE LATEST FOOTY NEWS & TRENDS, RED-HOT GOSSIP, ACE VIDEOS & EPIC BANTER!

facebook.com/
matchmagazine

youtube.com/matchymovie

twitter.com/
matchmagazine

snapchat.com/add/
matchmagazine

instagram.com/
matchmagofficial

EPIC WEBSITE: WWW.MATCHFOOTBALL.CO.UK

TAVERNIER

FACTPACK

Name: James Tavernier
D.O.B: 31 October, 1991
Position: Right-back
Country: England
Strongest Foot: Right
Top Skill: Lightning speed!
Boot Brand: Adidas

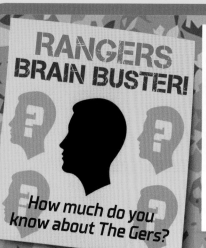

RANGERS BRAIN BUSTER!

How much do you know about The Gers?

1. How many Scottish League Cups have Rangers won?

2. What year were Rangers formed?

3. Which Rangers player is older – George Edmundson or Cedric Itten?

4. True or False? Rangers signed ace attacker Kemar Roofe from Leeds!

5. Can you name the national team that awesome midfielder Glen Kamara plays for?

6. What is the name of Rangers' training ground?

7. What round did Rangers get to in the 2019-20 Europa League?

8. Which player scored more goals in 2019-20 in all comps – Scott Arfield or Ryan Kent?

9. What boot brand does skipper James Tavernier wear?

10. True or False? One of Rangers' nicknames is 'The Teddy Bears'!

1 ....
2 ....
3 ....
4 ....
5 ....
6 ....
7 ....
8 ....
9 ....
10 ....

WORDFIT

Can you fit these Rangers legends into the giant grid below?

Archibald   Cairns   Durrant   Henderson   Little   McCulloch

Baxter   Cooper   English   Hubbard   McCloy   Novo

Brand   Cox   Goram   Jardine   McCoist   Souness

Brown   Cunningham   Gough   Johnstone   MacDonald   Thornton

Butcher   Davis   Greig   Laudrup   McPhail   Wilkins

ANSWERS ON PAGE 60

IBROX

Get the lowdown on the mind-blowing home of the Scottish giants!

THE NAME

The Gers' awesome stadium was named after the area of Glasgow it's located in – Ibrox! It was called Ibrox Park when it first opened, but became Ibrox Stadium after renovations were completed in 1997!

THE CAPACITY

A mind–blowing 118,567 people watched Rangers beat Celtic 2–1 back in 1939. While the capacity has decreased since then, it still remains one of the greatest stadiums in world football!

CLASSIC RANGERS MOMENTS

NO.2

FIORENTINA 0

RANGERS 0

0-0 ON AGGREGATE, RANGERS WIN 4-2 ON PENALTIES

Date: May 1, 2008

Stadium: Stadio Artemio Franchi, Florence

Competition: Europa League

What happened? Ten-man Rangers reached the Europa League final after beating Serie A giants Fiorentina on pens! Over two legs, neither team could break the deadlock after epic displays from both defences! In Florence, striker Daniel Cousin was sent off in extra time, but The Gers hung on for pens. Nacho Novo then scored the decisive spot kick, after Christian Vieri had missed for the home side. The scenes!

PENALTY SHOOTOUT STARS!

BIG '10

Test your knowledge of the greatest club in the world! Can you get all ten?

1 How old is awesome hitman Jermain Defoe – under 35 or over 35?

4 Which epic European trophy have Rangers won – the Cup Winners' Cup or Europa League?

2 What is the club's motto, which can be found on their badge?

3 True or False? Gers gaffer Steven Gerrard used to play for the club!

5 How many times did Gers legend Brian Laudrup win the Champions League?

6 How many goals did Alfredo Morelos score in the 2019–20 Europa League – 11, 14, 18 or 21?

7 Which three teams were in Rangers' tough Europa League group in the 2019–20 campaign?

8 How many times did Ally McCoist win the Scottish League Cup as a Gers player?

9 What is the base colour of Rangers' socks in 2020–21?

10 What is the name of Rangers' sick mascot?

1 point for each correct answer!

MY SCORE

/10

1. Jermain Defoe

2. Calvin Bassey

3. Cedric Itten

NAME THE CLUB

Can you name the clubs Rangers signed these top-class footballers from?

4. Ryan Kent

5. George Edmundson

6. Filip Helander

SPOT THE BALL!

Mark where you think the ball should be in this epic action pic!

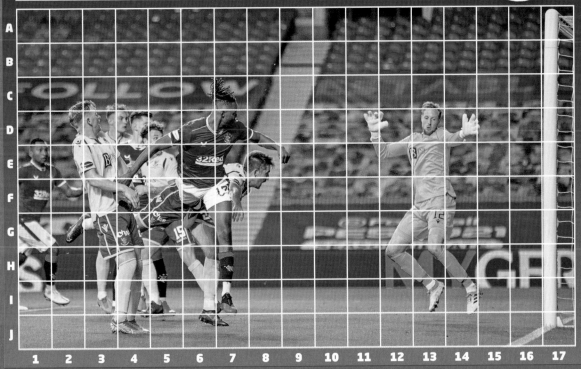

23

ANSWERS ON PAGE 60

DRAW YOUR FOOTY HERO!

RANGERS have some of the best players in the Scottish Premiership, so why not sketch your favourite superstar on the blank page?

24

KENT

FACTPACK

Name: Ryan Kent

D.O.B: 11 November, 1996

Position: Attacking midfielder

Country: England

Strongest Foot: Right

Top Skill: Dynamite dribbling!

Boot Brand: Nike

CHEERIO!

RANGERS FOOTBALL CLUB
READY

TWO IN A ROW

CELTIC	0
RANGERS	3

McCann 12, 76; Albertz 44 (pen)

Date: May 2, 1999

Stadium: Celtic Park, Glasgow

Competition: Scottish Premiership

What happened? Reigning league champs Celtic were dethroned of their title at home to arch-rivals Rangers! The Gers won the match 3-0 through a Neil McCann double and Jorg Albertz penalty, giving Rangers a first title victory at their rival's ground! Three players were sent off, too – two from Celtic and one from Rangers – as the game regularly boiled over! The result meant The Gers were league champions for the tenth time in 11 seasons. What a sick record!

PARTY AT THE PARK!

ICONIC KITS!

RANGERS have had some epic shirts during their wicked history – check out some of the real classics of the past!

STAR MAN
Nikica Jelavic
Goal machine Jelavic only made 20 league starts in 2010-11, but hit an epic 16 goals. Hero!

AWAY 2010-11

The last time Rangers won the Scottish Premiership title, they were wearing this awesome black kit as they thumped Kilmarnock 5-1! It was their first-ever all-black away kit, and it really oozed class! Since the 2010-11 season, they've had four further black away kits – Gers fans clearly love the classy look!

DID YOU KNOW?
Between 1986 and 2000, Rangers won the league title 12 times!

HOME 1996-97

Tons of top moments happened during the 1996-97 season! The Gers beat Celtic in all four league games, Denmark legend Brian Laudrup hit a mind-blowing 20 goals in all competitions and, of course, the club equalled The Hoops' record of winning nine league titles in a row! This kit really was victorious!

STAT ATTACK
Ally McCoist, Paul Gascoigne and Gordon Durie hit 62 goals between them in 1995-96!

AWAY 1995-96

A quality shirt required quality players, and that's exactly what Rangers had in 1995-96! Bagging a league and cup double, The Gers had a squad made up of Ally McCoist, Paul Gascoigne, Brian Laudrup, Gordon Durie and Richard Gough! It was one of Scottish footy's greatest teams to be assembled!

STAT ATTACK
In 1992-93, Rangers finished 13 points ahead of Celtic in the league!

HOME 1992-94

The 1992-94 jersey was Rangers' first to be made by footy brand Adidas, and what a beaut it was! It screams classic 90s footy shirts, with over the top white stripes and proper baggy sleeves! The Scottish giants won five trophies in the two seasons they wore it too, including the league title both times!

HOME 1997-99

We reckon Rangers fans have mixed memories of this Nike shirt! The first campaign they wore it, arch-rivals Celtic pipped them to the league title for the first time in ten seasons, while Hearts beat them in the Scottish Cup Final! Fast forward one season, and the club won the league title at Celtic Park wearing it. Sweet!

FAB FACT
Hitman Marco Negri bagged 23 goals in his first ten league games in 1997-98!

HOME 1994-96

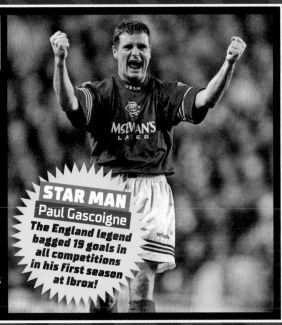

Rangers kits don't get much more iconic than this bad boy! The 1994-96 jersey was a proper Adidas classic, with three white stripes on the sleeves and an epic grandad-style collar! It was Gers legend Paul Gascoigne's first home shirt, with Rangers bagging three major trophies in the two seasons they wore it. Epic!

STAR MAN
Paul Gascoigne
The England legend bagged 19 goals in all competitions in his First season at Ibrox!

HOME 2007-08

This Umbro kit has been picked out for its bittersweet memories, rather than for its beauty! The Glasgow giants reached the Europa League Final back in 2008, but were beaten by Zenit 2-0! It was a quality run to the final in Manchester, with The Gers regularly wearing blue shorts and blue socks on the way. Legends!

FAB FACT
Rangers beat Dundee United in the 2008 Scottish League Cup Final wearing this shirt!

MORE CLASSY KITS!

HOME 1982-1984

AWAY 1996-97

HOME 1973-76

HOME 2002-03

DESIGN YOUR

HOME KIT

AWAY KIT

GERS KIT!

THIRD KIT

GOALKEEPER KIT

WORDSEARCH

Can you find the names of all these Gers players past and present?

```
U  X  G  O  L  D  S  O  N  G  F  R  I  C  K  S  E  N  O  A  K  D  A  D  Q  K  I  Z  A  X
F  S  V  O  U  L  T  S  B  Z  G  W  A  L  T  S  L  E  R  B  G  E  H  R  Y  S  V  P  R  B
G  O  G  G  G  F  X  L  J  R  K  H  G  X  X  V  Z  C  T  H  O  S  C  U  K  R  G  L  C  C
A  B  A  R  V  E  L  A  D  Z  E  L  O  U  F  A  O  Q  Y  R  Z  V  I  M  U  M  E  C  N  J
S  R  X  L  E  M  C  E  D  H  M  V  A  N  B  R  O  N  C  K  H  O  R  S  T  L  R  Y  U  U
L  O  P  V  J  C  S  X  E  I  A  X  R  A  Q  R  N  X  H  O  V  P  E  J  L  M  U  P  H  K
T  O  L  A  J  C  E  Z  S  M  E  D  E  B  O  E  R  B  X  Q  F  I  L  L  E  N  Z  W  W  X
L  F  A  C  A  U  N  B  T  F  I  P  N  G  G  W  P  O  Y  Z  R  N  E  W  Y  L  R  K  P  X
U  E  U  U  G  L  L  W  F  L  S  N  I  C  N  V  A  M  H  N  T  D  K  I  X  P  A  M  N  G
M  E  V  I  B  L  C  Q  E  R  L  C  I  M  U  F  K  G  B  I  U  A  T  H  Q  A  I  V  E  M
W  S  Z  Q  L  O  H  B  R  L  T  I  D  F  Y  S  S  H  T  W  I  V  C  I  H  M  I  Y  I  N
I  V  I  Z  J  C  B  K  C  F  A  L  B  E  R  T  Z  N  X  U  D  I  H  I  Q  M  X  R  W  C
H  K  Z  Y  A  H  H  I  J  R  Z  I  Z  L  R  E  E  I  F  H  R  S  S  P  I  J  G  Q  L  G
P  I  Z  F  M  D  H  I  L  H  Q  V  T  E  M  K  W  C  I  H  O  X  H  H  C  T  H  H  N  Z
W  V  Q  N  O  R  F  L  E  A  L  X  D  L  D  X  O  Y  E  F  S  I  Y  Y  T  D  W  B  O  Q
D  R  T  W  R  Z  E  N  B  S  F  N  W  A  K  Z  L  W  G  N  N  D  S  G  L  Y  R  N  N  Q
E  H  Z  H  U  V  R  C  A  X  A  F  F  O  G  Y  K  O  N  T  E  R  M  A  N  W  Q  H  K  B
X  K  N  G  S  R  G  E  Y  L  K  V  E  Z  W  Y  S  Y  W  S  F  L  E  V  H  Q  D  K  V  O
A  J  I  E  O  O  U  P  E  E  B  A  B  R  O  K  L  Z  I  J  Q  T  N  A  E  U  U  D  B  L
M  T  J  O  W  Z  S  H  M  D  I  P  I  S  T  Q  B  K  R  H  A  U  D  F  E  O  T  W  A  I
E  P  W  X  D  E  O  T  K  O  K  I  A  P  U  Y  S  Z  W  Q  B  E  E  F  X  R  F  B  L  L
V  G  C  C  S  N  N  G  H  R  L  T  L  F  Y  L  D  Q  X  H  S  N  S  O  X  C  V  M  L  T
V  A  Z  H  E  T  S  M  H  E  E  S  J  Z  E  R  N  T  H  D  F  G  H  G  D  J  H  E  W  N
Q  S  L  G  L  A  O  A  W  T  N  Z  T  H  F  U  Y  O  M  V  H  N  A  R  I  K  F  U  O  U
J  C  Z  L  F  L  K  S  R  N  N  D  C  F  V  N  G  V  A  D  B  X  G  W  N  F  V  G  Q  M
L  O  U  V  L  J  E  A  J  B  T  N  R  A  G  C  D  R  M  L  D  P  I  R  U  T  W  Z  K  A
T  I  A  B  O  D  J  Y  E  X  A  E  G  Y  I  Z  R  F  E  Z  X  G  X  B  W  W  H  K  F  N
P  G  Q  V  S  S  Y  P  M  K  T  M  Z  B  W  W  M  T  I  C  Q  E  J  J  G  F  F  F  P  W
X  N  E  D  U  V  L  K  L  E  Q  P  L  D  J  F  P  O  P  W  I  F  A  F  U  O  W  A  Y  P
G  E  Q  F  T  H  H  C  X  C  H  A  B  A  I  U  B  N  L  F  F  J  E  Q  J  X  G  C  R  W
```

Albertz	Buffel	Gascoigne	Kanchelskis	Mols
Amoruso	Davis	Goldson	Kent	Numan
Arteta	De Boer	Hagi	Konterman	Ricksen
Arveladze	Edu	Helander	Lafferty	Roofe
Ball	Ferguson	Hendry	McCulloch	Rozental
Boli	Flo	Jelavic	Mendes	Van Bronckhorst

ANSWERS ON PAGE 60

DEFOE

CLASSIC RANGERS MOMENTS NO. 4

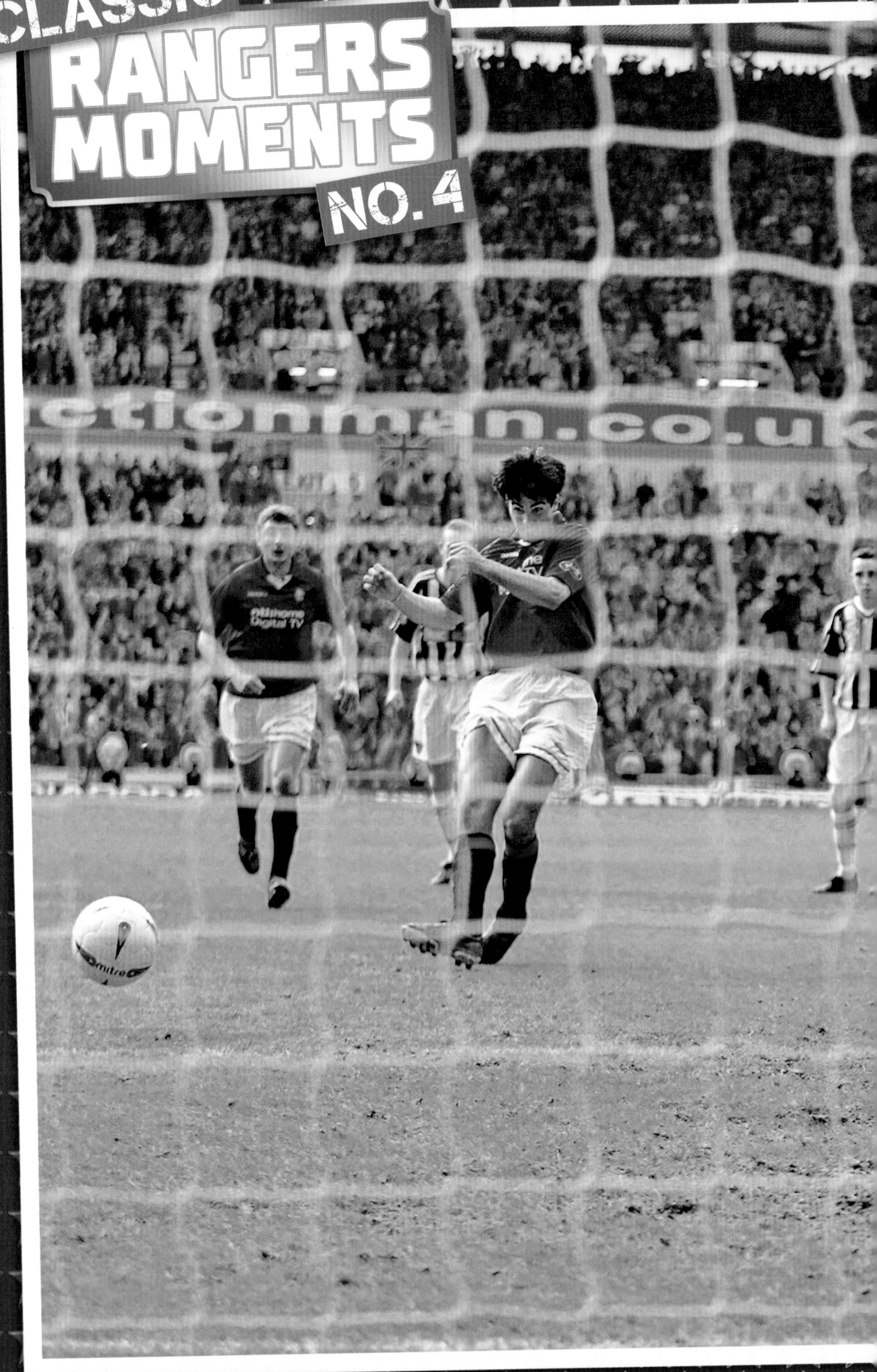

INJURY-TIME PEN SEALS THE TITLE!

RANGERS — 6
Mols 3; Caniggia 16; Arverladze 30; De Boer 65; Thompson 67; Arteta 93 (pen)

DUNFERMLINE — 1
Dair 11

Date: May 25, 2003

Stadium: Ibrox Stadium, Glasgow

Competition: Scottish Premiership

What happened? The end of the 2002–03 season is one of the most dramatic finishes in Scottish football history! Going into the final day, Rangers and Celtic were level on points with identical goal differences! On a super Sunday, The Hoops were 4–0 up at Kilmarnock, while The Gers were thrashing Dunfermline 5–1 at Ibrox going into injury time. Another Celtic goal would bag them the title, but Mikel Arteta and co. had other ideas! The CM hit a 93rd-minute pen to secure the title for the home side!

2020-21 FIRST TEAM SQUAD

GOALKEEPERS

No.	Player	League Games/Goals 2019-20	Signed from
1	Allan McGregor	27/0	Hull, 2018
13	Andy Firth	0/0	Barrow AFC, 2019
33	Jon McLaughlin	N/A	Sunderland, 2020

MIDFIELDERS

No.	Player	League Games/Goals 2019-20	Signed from
7	Ianis Hagi	7/1	Genk, 2020
8	Ryan Jack	19/4	Aberdeen, 2017
10	Steven Davis	24/0	Southampton, 2019
14	Ryan Kent	21/7	Liverpool, 2019
15	Jamie Murphy	2/0	Brighton, 2018
17	Joe Aribo	27/3	Charlton, 2019
18	Glen Kamara	19/0	Dundee, 2019
21	Brandon Barker	6/1	Man. City, 2019
22	Jordan Jones	7/0	Kilmarnock, 2019
37	Scott Arfield	26/5	Burnley, 2018
40	Glenn Middleton	N/A	Norwich, 2018

Leon Balogun

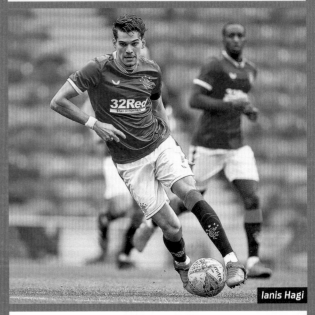

Ianis Hagi

DEFENDERS

No.	Player	League Games/Goals 2019-20	Signed from
2	James Tavernier	24/3	Wigan, 2015
3	Calvin Bassey	N/A	Leicester, 2020
4	George Edmundson	7/1	Oldham, 2019
5	Filip Helander	8/1	Bologna, 2019
6	Connor Goldson	29/3	Brighton, 2018
16	Nathan Patterson	0/0	Academy
19	Nikola Katic	19/2	NK Slaven, 2018
26	Leon Balogun	N/A	Wigan, 2020
31	Borna Barisic	22/2	NK Osijek, 2018

FORWARDS

No.	Player	League Games/Goals 2019-20	Signed from
9	Jermain Defoe	20/13	Bournemouth, 2020
11	Cedric Itten	N/A	St. Gallen, 2020
20	Alfredo Morelos	26/12	HJK Helsinki, 2017
24	Greg Stewart	16/3	Birmingham, 2019
25	Kemar Roofe	N/A	Anderlecht, 2020

MEET THE MANAGER

STEVEN GERRARD

Get the complete lowdown on the man in charge of RANGERS!

THE PLAYER

Top players don't always make great managers, but Gerrard is slowly proving he's one of the best exceptions to that rule. As Liverpool's midfield king, Stevie was one of the greatest box-to-box midfielders of the 21st century. His Man of the Match performance in the 2005 CL Final for The Reds is legendary, and he's considered by many experts to be the Anfield club's best ever player.

RETIREMENT

After hanging up his boots in 2016, Gerrard set about completing his coaching badges. He was quickly appointed as a youth coach in Liverpool's academy, taking charge of their U18s and U19s. After just over a year in The Reds' youth setup, the England hero took over as the new Gers gaffer on June 1, 2018!

GERS GAFFER

In 2018-19, his first season in charge, Gerrard guided the club to second – their highest top-flight finish since 2012! In the following campaign, The Gers finished second again, but this time enjoyed an extended run in the Europa League. The Scottish giants reached the Round of 16, losing to Bayer Leverkusen over two legs. The 40-year-old could be the first long-term manager Rangers have had for a number of years!

GERS S[T]

We've got some epic inside information you might not already know about your favourite Rangers heroes!

BALOGUN

The top centre-back was born in Germany, but plays for Nigeria at international level!

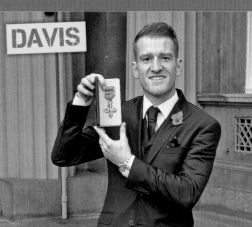

BARISIC

The Gers left-back loves F1, and has even been to a race!

Check out some Instagram pics From Rangers' top stars on p. 50!

DAVIS

CM Davis was given an MBE back in 2017 for services to football. Legend!

STEWART

Stewart left Rangers back in 2003 aged 13, then rejoined the club 16 years later in 2019!

DEFOE

Hitman Defoe went vegan a few years ago, but then gave up after accidentally eating fish!

ROOFE

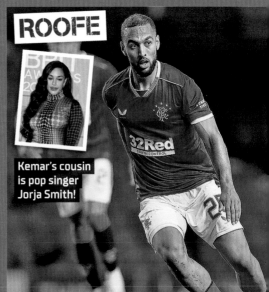

Kemar's cousin is pop singer Jorja Smith!

ARS revealed!

JONES

The wicked winger loves a bit of fishing! Look at the size of that fish!

TAVERNIER

The right-back was part of Leeds' academy as a youngster, and played a season as a goalkeeper before moving to midfield!

HAGI

Ianis' dad is legendary footballer Gheorghe Hagi – he played for both Real Madrid and Barcelona during a 19-year career!

JACK

The sick DM's first-ever league match was actually against Rangers! He made his Scottish Premiership debut for Aberdeen back in 2010!

GERRARD

The gaffer is a keen golfer – he loves playing a round when he gets the chance!

BASSEY

At international level, Bassey could play for either Italy, Nigeria or England!

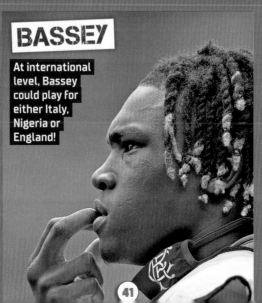

McGREGOR

GK McGregor was best man at ex-Gers player Alan Hutton's wedding!

SPOT THE DIFFERENCE

Study these Rangers v Bayer Leverkusen pictures carefully,
then see if you can find the ten differences between them!

HAGI

FACTPACK

Name: Ianis Hagi

D.O.B: 22 October, 1998

Position: Attacking midfielder

Country: Romania

Strongest Foot: Right

Top Skill: Sick ball control!

Boot Brand: Nike

"Ooh la la! The atmosphere at Ibrox is absolutely magical. To my way of appreciating football, it's truly really beautiful. That's how to support your team!"

It's fair to say Didier Drogba's experience of Ibrox in 2007 left a lasting impression!

"I know the atmosphere that's generated here, and that makes it tough for any team. I thought the fans were unbelievable again."

Thierry Henry said this after a Champions League game between Rangers and Barcelona back in 2007!

HE SAID WHAT?

"I'll play for Rangers as long as I can, then spend the rest of my life being depressed."

Ally McCoist never wanted his Rangers career to ever end. Neither did the fans, Ally!

Get a load of some of our fave Rangers quotes of all time!

"Glasgow Rangers. God I loved playing for them."

Paul Gascoigne was loved by Rangers fans during his three-year spell at the club!

"In Scotland, I'm more fond of Glasgow Rangers. There was a great winger who played for them called Willie Henderson."

Football legend Eusebio liked The Gers more than Celtic. What a hero!

"When I play, I am like a soldier going into battle. My team-mates are my comrades. We will never give up, no matter the opposition."

Dado Prso would run through walls for Rangers!

SUBSCRIBE TO MATCH! & GET THIS EPIC GIFT!*

AWESOME BOOMPODS SPEAKER WORTH £34.99!

SAVE OVER 30% ON THE SHOP PRICE!

PACKED EVERY WEEK WITH...

★ Cool gear & quizzes

★ Interviews & stats

★ Megastars & more!

HOW TO SUBSCRIBE TO MATCH!

CALL
01959 543 747
QUOTE: MATAN21

ONLINE
SHOP.KELSEY.CO.UK/
MATAN21

RANGERS
GREATEST OLD FIRM MOMENTS!

Check out some of RANGERS' best-ever moments against their massive rivals Celtic!

GERS' FOUR-YEAR WAIT!
Rangers 2-2 Celtic
Rangers win 5-4 on penalties
Scottish Cup, 2016

This match will live long in the memory for Rangers fans! The club had spent four seasons outside of the Scottish Premiership between 2012 and 2016, and won promotion back to the top flight a couple of weeks before this fixture. To then beat Celtic for the first time in four years to reach the Scottish Cup final was the real icing on the cake that month. Legends!

SUPER STEVEN DAVIS!
Rangers 1-0 Celtic
Scottish Premiership, 2009

This Rangers victory almost certainly sealed the 2008–09 league title for the Glasgow giants! In a tight match, a first-half tap in from midfielder Steven Davis proved to be the difference! The win meant Rangers overtook Celtic in the table with three matches to play!

PERFECT PETER!
Celtic 2-3 Rangers
Scottish Cup, 2002

Peter Lovenkrands played over 175 times for the Glasgow giants, and this game was arguably his greatest in a Gers shirt! The Hoops twice took the lead in the Scottish Cup final, but Lovenkrands hit the first equaliser, and Barry Ferguson grabbed the second! Peter then bagged the winner in the 90th minute, sending Rangers fans crazy at Hampden Park!

BHOYS BASHING!
Rangers 5-1 Celtic
Scottish Premiership, 1988

This 5-1 win for Rangers marked a changing of the guard in Scotland – The Gers had won just one league title in the previous ten seasons, with Celtic bagging five in the same period! Ally McCoist hit a dynamite double, setting Rangers on their way to nine Scottish Premiership titles in a row!

HIGH FIVE!
Rangers 5-1 Celtic
Scottish Premiership, 2000

Celtic were massive favourites going into this one – they were 15 points clear of Rangers in the league, and had already beaten their arch rivals 6-2 earlier in the season! The Gers were out for revenge though, as they put five past Celtic with five different goalscorers! One of the net-busters was £12 million man Tore Andre Flo on his debut!

THE SHAME GAME!
Celtic 0–3 Rangers
Scottish Premiership, 1999

We've already mentioned on page 28 how mad this game was on the pitch, as Rangers bagged the title at Celtic Park, but what we didn't mention were the terrible scenes off it! Referee Hugh Dallas was hit by an object from the stands, fans invaded the pitch, and then they clashed with Gers players after the final whistle. Ten players were booked too, in a match named 'The Shame Game'!

STEVEN'S SCOTTISH GIANTS!
Celtic 1–2 Rangers
Scottish Premiership, 2019

While Rangers didn't end up beating Celtic to the 2019-20 title, this game will always mean a lot to Rangers supporters! It was an epic battle between the two Scottish giants, as The Gers went to within two points of their arch rivals at the top of the Scottish Premiership! You can read more about this awesome game on page 54!

YOUTH CUP MADNESS!
Rangers U17s 3–2 Celtic U17s
Glasgow Cup, 2013

You might be wondering why we're featuring an Under-17s match, but we reckon it shows how big the Old Firm derby really is! Around 6,000 fans attended this academy match, with pitch invasions, crowd trouble and flares thrown onto the pitch throughout! The two fans really don't get on!

OLD FIRM FIRSTS!
Rangers 1–0 Celtic
Scottish Premiership, 2018

This game had a series of Old Firm firsts – it was The Gers' first victory over Celtic in the league since returning to the top flight, a first derby-day defeat for Hoops gaffer Brendan Rodgers in 13 games, and a first victory for Steven Gerrard over Celtic!

SCOTTISH CUP SUPERSTARS!
Rangers 1–0 Celtic
Scottish Cup, 1999

It seemed fitting that Rangers would end up winning the last Scottish Cup of the 90s, having won the trophy three times already that decade! The 1-0 victory over Celtic at a fully renovated Hampden Park took the club to 28 Scottish Cup triumphs in total, just two behind their Glasgow neighbours!

STAT ATTACK!

Get a load of *RANGERS*' biggest signings, mega trophy cabinet, record goalscorers, social media followers and loads more!

FIVE BIGGEST SIGNINGS

	PLAYER	YEAR	FEE
1	Tore Andre Flo	2000	£12m
2	Ryan Kent	2019	£7m
3	Michael Ball	2001	£6.5m
4	Mikel Arteta	2002	£6m
5	G. van Bronckhorst	1998	£5.5m

FIVE BIGGEST SALES

	PLAYER	YEAR	FEE
1	Alan Hutton	2008	£9m
2	G. van Bronckhorst	2001	£8.5m
3	Jean-Alain Boumsong	2005	£8m
4	Carlos Cuellar	2008	£7.8m
5	Barry Ferguson	2003	£7.5m

MAJOR TROPHIES

54	33	27	1
Scottish Premierships	Scottish Cups	Scottish League Cups	European Cup Winners' Cup

ALL-TIME TOP SCORERS

Player	Goals
Ally McCoist 1983-1998	355
Bob McPhail 1927-1940	261
Jimmy Smith 1930-1946	249
Jimmy Fleming 1925-1934	220
Derek Johnstone 1970-1983 & 1984-1985	210
Ralph Brand 1954-1965	206
Willie Reid 1909-1920	195
Willie Thornton 1936-1954	194
Robert C. Hamilton 1897-1908	184
Andy Cunningham 1914-1929	182

11

In 1994-95, lethal finisher Gordon Durie scored the fastest goal in Rangers history! It took him just 11 seconds to bag against Dundee United!

CHAMPIONS LEAGUE RECORD
ALL-TIME

PLAYED	WON
161	**62**

LOST	DRAWN
59	**40**

GOALS	CONCEDED
232	**218**

ALL-TIME APPEARANCE MAKERS

- Ian McColl **526**
- John Greig **755**
- Peter McCloy **535**
- Sandy Jardine **674**
- Davie Cooper **540**
- Ally McCoist **581**
- Derek Johnstone **546**
- Sandy Archibald **580**
- Dougie Gray **555**
- David Meiklejohn **563**

7

Hitman Alfredo Morelos became the first Gers player to score in seven consecutive matches in 2018-19!

13 COUNTRIES REPRESENTED IN 2019-20 SQUAD

Canada

Colombia Croatia England Finland

Nigeria N. Ireland Romania Scotland

Sweden Switzerland USA Wales

BIGGEST VICTORIES

ALL-TIME	EUROPEAN
13-0	**10-0**
v Possilpark, 1877*	v Valletta, 1983

*Also beat two other teams 13-0

VALLETTA F.C.

facebook
690k+ LIKES

410k+ FOLLOWERS

twitter
551k+ FOLLOWERS

Insta RANGERS

 greegsy1

86k+ followers

The GK took on the toilet roll keepy-uppy challenge during lockdown. LOL!

 stevengerrard

9m+ followers

The Gers gaffer turned 40 in May, 2020! You're getting old, boss!

 ryanjack_8

43k+ followers

Jack won The Gers' Player of the Season award for 2019-20!

rangersfc

410k+ followers

Check out bucket hat Bassey modelling this season's away kit!

nikolakatic2

90k+ followers

After having knee surgery, Nikola went to Croatia to recover!

jamestavernier2

128k+ followers

Check out the world's tallest building behind Tavernier. Wowzers!

 iamjermaindefoe

518k+ followers

Defoe signed for the club on a permanent basis in January!

 georgeedmundson__

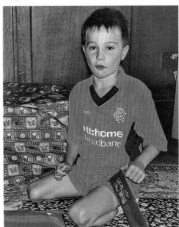

48k+ followers

George shared this pic of himself in a Gers away kit from 2002-03!

 jamiebarjonas_

29k+ followers

The CM went up Ben A'an with some mates during the summer!

 leonbalogun

98k+ followers

Leon took this pic on moving day after joining the club in July!

 alfredomorelos30

185k+ followers

Yes, this is an awesome picture – but how did Rangers goal machine Alfredo get his Lamborghini into Ibrox?

ACTION REPLAY

How much do you remember about last season's awesome victory over Celtic at Celtic Park?

1 Rangers beat Celtic, but what was the final score?

2 Which of these players didn't get booked – Katic, Barisic, Morelos or Aribo?

3 Who hit the opening goal – Edouard or Kent?

4 How many corners were there in total – under 10 or over 10?

5 Who played in net for The Gers – Allan McGregor or Wes Foderingham?

6 How many shots were there by both teams in total – 18, 28, 38 or 48?

7 Which team had more possession?

8 Who was subbed on first for Rangers – Arfield or Edmundson?

ANSWERS ON PAGE 60

BROXI BEAR

FACTPACK

Name: *Broxi Bear*

Age: *13 November, 1993*

Position: *Mascot*

Country: *Scotland*

Strongest Foot: *Both*

Top Skill: *Being a bear!*

Boot Brand: *New Bear-lance*

RANGERS MOMENTS
NO.5

CELTIC	1
Edouard 41	

RANGERS	2
Kent 36; Katic 56	

Date: December 29, 2019

Stadium: Celtic Park, Glasgow

Competition: Scottish Premiership

What happened? Rangers went to within two points of Celtic at the top of the table, after beating The Hoops 2-1 at Celtic Park! Ryan Kent made the home side pay for missing a 32nd-minute penalty, coolly slotting home from inside the box four minutes later! Odsonne Edouard equalised for Celtic just before half-time, but Rangers were back in front early in the second half through a thumping Nikola Katic header! It was the Scottish giants' first victory at Celtic Park for over nine years!

NINE-YEAR WAIT ENDED!

Pick your five favourite Gers stars, send them to MATCH and you could win a mega prize!

COMPETITION

WIN! A FREE ONE-YEAR MATCH SUBSCRIPTION

PICK YOUR TOP 5 GERS HEROES!

For the chance to win this mind-blowing magazine subscription, just write down your five favourite Rangers players, fill out your contact details and email a photograph of this page to **match.magazine@kelsey.co.uk.** Closing date: January 31, 2021. What are you waiting for?

1.

2.

3.

4.

5.

NAME:

DATE OF BIRTH:

ADDRESS:

MOBILE:

EMAIL:

Jermain Defoe

Kenny Miller

Kris Boyd

Steven Naismith

ODD ONE OUT!

Which of these lethal goal machines wasn't born in Scotland?

Steven Thompson

Ross McCormack

5 QUESTIONS ON...

IBROX

RANGERS F.C.

1 What is Ibrox Stadium's wicked capacity - over 50,000 or under 50,000?

2 When was Ibrox first opened - 1889, 1899, 1909, 1919 or 1929?

3 Which epic city is the world-class stadium located in - Edinburgh, Glasgow or Dundee?

4 What did Ibrox used to be called - Ibrox Park, Ibrox Bridge, Ibrox Field or Ibrox Parade?

5 True or False? The stadium hosted rugby sevens matches as part of the Commonwealth Games held in 2014!

NAME THE TEAM

The players from Rangers' 2019 Europa League away match against Porto are hiding – can you work out who they are?

1. Left-back

2. Centre-back

3. Centre-back

4. Midfielder

5. Goalkeeper

6. Attacking midfielder

7. Right-back

8. Midfielder

9. Midfielder

10. Striker

11. Attacking midfielder

ANSWERS ON PAGE 60

Brain-Buster P16

1. 27
2. 1872
3. Cedric Itten
4. False
5. Finland
6. Auchenhowie
7. Round of 16
8. Scott Arfield
9. Adidas
10. True

Big 10 P22

1. Over 35
2. Ready
3. False
4. Cup Winners' Cup
5. Once
6. 14
7. Feyenoord, Porto and Young Boys
8. Nine times
9. Black
10. Broxi Bear

Name The Club P23

1. Bournemouth
2. Leicester
3. St. Gallen
4. Liverpool
5. Oldham
6. Bologna

Spot The Ball P23

F16

Wordfit P17

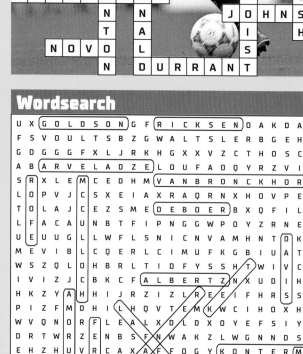

(Crossword grid answers include: MCCLOY, BAXTER, HUBBARD, CAIRNS, CUNNINGHAM, MCPHAIL, BROWN, LITTLE, WILKINS, GORAM, SOUNESS, GREIG, COX, MCCULLOCH, HENDERSON, JOHNSTONE, NOVO, DURRANT, BRAND, LUDRUP, JARDINE, MACDONALD)

Wordsearch P34

(Word search grid with answers including: GOLDSON, RICKSEN, ARVELADZE, VAN BRONCKHORST, DEBOER, ALBERT, KONTERMAN, EDU)

Spot The Difference P42

Action Replay P52

1. Celtic 1–2 Rangers
2. Joe Aribo
3. Ryan Kent
4. Over 10
5. Allan McGregor
6. 28
7. Celtic
8. Scott Arfield

Odd One Out P58

Jermain Defoe

Ibrox Quiz P58

1. Over 50,000
2. 1899
3. Glasgow
4. Ibrox Park
5. True

Name The Team P59

1. Borna Barisic
2. Connor Goldson
3. Filip Helander
4. Ryan Jack
5. Allan McGregor
6. Brandon Barker
7. James Tavernier
8. Glen Kamara
9. Steven Davis
10. Alfredo Morelos
11. Ryan Kent

ROLL OF HONOUR

EUROPEAN CUP WINNERS' CUP
1971-72

SCOTTISH PREMIERSHIP
1890-91, 1898-99, 1899-1900, 1900-01, 1901-02, 1910-11, 1911-12, 1912-13, 1917-18, 1919-20, 1920-21, 1922-23, 1923-24, 1924-25, 1926-27, 1927-28, 1928-29, 1929-30, 1930-31, 1932-33, 1933-34, 1934-35, 1936-37, 1938-39, 1946-47, 1948-49, 1949-50, 1952-53, 1955-56, 1956-57, 1958-59, 1960-61, 1962-63, 1963-64, 1974-75, 1975-76, 1977-78, 1986-87, 1988-89, 1989-90, 1990-91, 1991-92, 1992-93, 1993-94, 1994-95, 1995-96, 1996-97, 1998-99, 1999-2000, 2002-03, 2004-05, 2008-09, 2009-10, 2010-11

SCOTTISH CHAMPIONSHIP
2015-16

SCOTTISH LEAGUE ONE
2013-14

SCOTTISH LEAGUE TWO
2012-13

SCOTTISH CUP
1893-94, 1896-97, 1897-98, 1902-03, 1927-28, 1929-30, 1931-32, 1933-34, 1934-35, 1935-36, 1947-48, 1948-49, 1949-50, 1952-53, 1959-60, 1961-62, 1962-63, 1963-64, 1965-66, 1972-73, 1975-76, 1977-78, 1978-79, 1980-81, 1991-92, 1992-93, 1995-96, 1998-99, 1999-2000, 2001-02, 2002-03, 2007-08, 2008-09

SCOTTISH LEAGUE CUP
1946-47, 1948-49, 1960-61, 1961-62, 1963-64, 1964-65, 1970-71, 1975-76, 1977-78, 1978-79, 1981-82, 1983-84, 1984-85, 1986-87, 1987-88, 1988-89, 1990-91, 1992-93, 1993-94, 1996-97, 1998-99, 2001-02, 2002-03, 2004-05, 2007-08, 2009-10, 2010-11

SCOTTISH CHALLENGE CUP
2015-16

EMERGENCY WAR LEAGUE
1939-40

EMERGENCY WAR CUP
1939-40

SOUTHERN LEAGUE
1940-41, 1941-42, 1942-43, 1943-44, 1944-45, 1945-46

SOUTHERN LEAGUE CUP
1940-41, 1941-42, 1942-43, 1944-45

GLASGOW LEAGUE
1895-96, 1897-98

GLASGOW CUP
1893, 1894, 1897, 1898, 1900, 1901, 1902, 1911, 1912, 1913, 1914, 1918, 1919, 1922, 1923, 1924, 1925, 1930, 1932, 1933, 1934, 1936, 1937, 1938, 1940, 1942, 1943, 1944, 1945, 1948, 1950, 1954, 1957, 1958, 1960, 1969, 1971, 1975, 1976, 1979, 1983, 1985, 1986, 1987

VICTORY CUP
1946

SUMMER CUP
1942

GLASGOW MERCHANTS CHARITY CUP
1878-79, 1896-97, 1899-1900, 1903-04, 1905-06, 1906-07, 1908-09, 1910-11, 1918-19, 1921-22, 1922-23, 1924-25, 1927-28, 1928-29, 1929-30, 1930-31, 1931-32, 1932-33, 1933-34, 1938-39, 1939-40, 1940-41, 1941-42, 1943-44, 1944-45, 1945-46, 1946-47, 1947-48, 1950-51, 1954-55, 1956-57, 1959-60